Tractors

Tom Streissguth

Capstone Press

MINNEAPOLIS

LB wf yb BL

Printed in the United States of America.

Capstone Press • 2440 Fernbrook Lane • Minneapolis, MN 55447

Editorial Director   John Coughlan
Managing Editor   John Martin
Production Editor   James Stapleton

Photo Credits: Deere & Company: pp. 4, 8-9, 17, 18, 22-23, 27; Ford/New Holland: pp. 13, 33; Globe Photos: pp. 10, 14, 39, 41; J.I.Case: pp. 7, 24, 28, 30; Randy Leffingwell: pp. 19, 20, 21, 25, 32, 34, 37, 40.

Library of Congress Cataloging-in-Publication Data

Streissguth, Thomas, 1958-
  Tractors / by Thomas Streissguth
    p. cm. -- (Cruisin')
  Includes bibliographical references and index.
  ISBN 1-56065-254-3
  1. Farm tractors--Juvenile literature. [1. Tractors.]
  I. Title. II. Series
  TL233.5.S77   1996
  629.225--dc20   95-7121
                                                          CIP

99 98 97 96 95   6 5 4 3 2 1

13.35

Table of Contents

Chapter 1   The Machine that Works 5

Chapter 2   Steam Tractors and Gasoline

Tractors 11

Chapter 3   More Tractor History 15

Chapter 4   Tractor Makers 29

Chapter 5   Driverless Tractors 39

Glossary 43

To Learn More 46

Some Useful Addresses 47

Index 48

Chapter 1

The Machine that Works

There's a lot of hard work to do on a farm. Before growing any crops, you have to break up the earth, dig up tree stumps, and move heavy rocks out of the fields. After planting the seeds, you have to keep the fields clear of weeds. You have to spread **fertilizer** to help the crop grow. Then comes the biggest job of all–harvesting.

A hundred years ago, you would have used horses, and your own muscles, to do these jobs. Even with the help of horses, farming was a lot of work.

Farming is still a lot of work. But tractors have made the job much easier. Modern tractors can pull all kinds of tools and **implements**. They don't get tired or hungry, like horses do. And if they're maintained, they will run forever.

Tractors and Implements

The tractor is the machine the farmer uses most often. To grow and harvest a crop, the farmer attaches different implements to the tractor. These include plows, planters, cultivators, harvesters, balers, and mowers. Each implement has an important job to do.

With the help of tractors, farmers can now plow, seed, and harvest crops on much larger farms. They can grow crops in poor soil, and in places where they couldn't plant in the past. And their harvests are getting bigger and bigger. Tractors are helping many farmers earn a good living.

Over the last century, there have been many improvements to the tractor. The designs of engines, cabs, and transmissions are always

Tractors can help the farmer plow fields and prepare the ground for planting.

changing. Implements are more powerful, and can do more of the heavy work. As a result, modern tractors are probably the most useful machines in the world.

With a special attachment, this tractor can carry a heavy tank of liquid fertilizer

Chapter 2

Steam Tractors and Gasoline Tractors

The first farming engines were steam engines. These machines powered different kinds of equipment with a system of pulleys and belts. But the early steam tractors were not self-propelled. To move them, the farmer had to hitch them to a team of horses.

Self-Propelled Tractors

The first self-propelled tractors appeared in the 1850s. Mostly, farmers used them to plow the soil. These tractors were powered by steam, and they were heavy, slow, and dangerous. To create the steam, a wood or coal fire heated a big water boiler. A crew had to feed the fire, carefully control the steam pressure, and watch out for sparks.

Gasoline Tractors

John Froehlich, an Iowa blacksmith, built the first gasoline-powered farm engine in the 1890s. This machine used an **internal-combustion engine** and weighed 9,000 pounds (4.08 metric tons).

Gasoline and steam tractors worked side by side for a few years. But in 1901, Charles Hart and Charles Parr introduced huge gasoline tractors that were a big success among farmers.

The Hart-Parr machines weighed 20,000 pounds (9.07 metric tons). But they worked better than the old steam tractors. The first competition between steam tractors and gasoline tractors took place in Canada at Winnipeg, Manitoba, in 1908. The gasoline tractors won.

This old tractor uses heavy steel wheels. During the 1930s, the first rubber tires for tractors were made.

Many companies were soon making gasoline tractors. The Ford Motor Company made the most popular machines. In 1917, Henry Ford produced the first Fordson tractor. This tractor was much lighter than its rivals. Farmers bought more Fordsons than all other tractor models combined during the 1920s.

Chapter 3

More Tractor History

Over the years, a series of inventions gradually improved the tractor. These improvements made the farmer's many jobs much easier.

The Power Takeoff

The **power takeoff**, or PTO, was invented in 1918. It transfers power from the engine to the implement attached to the tractor. It does this through a **driveshaft**. The PTO's shaft comes in two parts that can slide together. This allows the shaft to get longer and shorter. There are flexible joints at both ends of the shaft.

This design allows the tractor to take sharp turns and cross rough ground while pulling and powering an implement. Most PTOs can also run implements when the tractor is not moving.

Tractor companies measure PTOs by their **horsepower**. The more horsepower the PTO delivers to the implement, the more powerful the tractor.

The Drawbar

Later, a **drawbar** was invented. Farmers used this device to attach implements to the back of the tractor. The drawbars had a standard size and width, so farmers could use many different kinds of implements with their tractors.

Row-Crop Tractors

In the 1920s, the first **row-crop tractors** appeared. The front wheels of these new models sat under the center of the tractor. On some models, the farmer could change the width of the front and rear axles.

The wheels of this tractor are just wide enough to allow the farmer to work two rows of crops.

This allowed farmers to **cultivate** crops like beans and corn that were planted in rows. It also made it easier to make tight turns at the end of the rows. International Harvester's Farmall tractor was one of the first and best row-crop tractors.

The powerful traction of the big rear wheels allows tractors to haul heavy loads.

The Hitch

Before heading out to the fields, the farmer hooks heavy equipment to the tractor's hitch. The **three-point hitch**, the most common hitch, was invented by Henry Ferguson in the 1930s.

On a three-point hitch, two lower links sit under the tractor's rear axle. An upper link sits above the axle. The hitch moves up and down while the tractor travels over the field. The farmer can raise and lower the hitch with a button or lever.

The hitch transfers the weight of the implement to the rear wheels of the tractor. This way, the wheels gain **traction** and the tractor can pull the implements without using a lot of engine power.

This Minneapolis Moline tractor was one of the first to offer a closed cab.

New Tires and Tracks

The first tractors had heavy steel wheels. Their weight pressed down hard on the soil, and they didn't get much traction. This made it hard to plow and cultivate the soil.

In the 1930s, the first rubber tires for tractors created a revolution in farming. They were much lighter than steel, yet their bumpy surfaces got more traction than steel wheels

Older tractors weren't very comfortable, but they were tough. Many are still in use.

did. Farmers sometimes added water to their rubber tires for more traction on muddy or sandy ground.

Hydraulic Power Systems

Many tractors began using new hydraulic power systems in the 1940s. A **hydraulic system** is made up of fluid-filled cylinders that the engine operates through a pump. The tractor's hydraulics raise and lower implements through the hitch. They can also move weight

The QuadTrack tractor runs on four endless tracks.

from the front wheels of the tractor to the back wheels, giving more traction in the back, where it is needed.

Hydraulics also provide power steering and power brakes. These systems make it much easier to drive the tractor over rough ground. A hydraulic pump can even raise or lower the driver's seat. This helps the farmer to see what he's doing more easily.

Crawler Tractors

Some tractors have steel tracks that loop around sets of wheels on the sides of the tractor. These are called **crawler tractors**, or caterpillars.

The caterpillar's driver steers by changing the speed of one of the tracks. If he wants to turn left, he slows down the left track. If he wants to turn right, he slows down the right track.

Caterpillars provide more traction than wheeled tractors.

Crawler tractors are used whenever a lot of traction is needed. They are slower than rubber-tired tractors. But they work much better than wheeled tractors on muddy, soft, or sandy soil. They spread the weight of the tractor over a larger surface.

With a bulldozer plow, caterpillars can move huge piles of earth. This makes them useful for construction or road-building. They can log large trees, carry heavy loads, and move up and down steep slopes.

Four-Wheel-Drive Tractors

Tractors with four-wheel drive get extra horsepower to the power takeoff. But four-wheel-drive machines are also much heavier than the normal, two-wheel-drive tractors.

Today's Tractors

The latest tractors combine power and usefulness. They can drive newer kinds of implements, such as sprayers, that have been invented to make the farmer's job easier.

The power takeoff mechanism allows tractors to operate machinery while they are standing still.

Today's tractors are also more comfortable for the driver. Many new models have air-conditioned cabs, power steering, and power brakes. Safety devices such as roll bars in the cab protect the farmer in case of a rollover.

A new tractor is expensive. Farmers spend a lot of money to buy a good one because they depend on their machines to stay in business.

Chapter 4
Tractor Makers

A few companies have earned reputations as the best manufacturers of tractors. Among them are the J.I. Case Company, Deere and Company, Ford Motor Company, Caterpillar Company, Massey-Ferguson, and the Allis-Chalmers Company. Here are some of their best-known models, from the past as well as the present.

Allis-Chalmers

Allis-Chalmers, like many other large companies, makes a line of tractors, not just a single model. The Allis-AGCO tractors have from 40 to 195 power-takeoff horsepower.

With a front loader attached, a tractor can do the tough chores around the barnyard.

The transmission system is an important part of a tractor. Farmers have to work at various speeds with different implements to do different jobs. AGCO tractors have a **synchronized transmission** and a **shuttle-shift reverser**. These let the driver quickly change from forward to reverse gears. The smaller AGCO models have **creeper gears**. These allow the tractor to work at very slow speeds.

J. I. Case

The J.I. Case Threshing Machine Company began building massive steam-powered tractors in the 1840s. In 1916, the company first brought out the Crossmotor tractors. On these models, the engine was mounted across the chassis, instead of lengthwise. The Crossmotor tractors were made of heavy cast iron. They developed about 11 horsepower.

The D-series Case tractors appeared in 1939. Painted a bright red, these machines came in different versions for orchards, vineyards, row crops, and industrial use.

J. I. Case is still an important tractor-manufacturing company. In 1987, Case brought out the 7200 series of Magnum tractors. These machines start at 130 PTO horsepower and go up to 215 PTO horsepower on the large Magnum 7250 tractor.

Caterpillar

Caterpillar is one of the world's largest makers of tractor, trucks, and heavy-construction equipment.

The Challenger 45 is one of Caterpillar's tracked row-crop tractors. These machines use endless tracks instead of rubber tires. They cause little damage to the soil, and they don't use as much fuel as some other tractors because they're lighter. Tracked machines are becoming more and more popular among farmers.

The Challenger 65 and 85 are tracked machines. The powerful Challenger 85C has 355 horsepower.

Tractors can haul heavy equipment, like this cultivator, along the crop rows.

Ford

Ford made some of the first large tractors. The Fordson tractor of the 1920s was one of the most popular models ever built. By the 1990s, the company was building tractors with engines as small as 12 horsepower and as large as 400 horsepower.

One of Ford's models is the Genesis 70 tractor manufactured in Canada at Winnipeg,

Ford has been a leading tractor manufacturer for many decades. This 501 Offset Workmaster from the 1950s was designed for work in vineyards and orchards.

Manitoba. The Genesis has new hydraulics and a new transmission system.

The Genesis 70 also has a new front axle. The axle, called the SuperSteer, moves the inside turning wheel outward while the tractor turns. This way the tractor can turn in a tight circle. Because the Genesis 70 doesn't need much room to turn at the end of a row, the farmer can plant longer rows.

John Deere

It's easy to spot a John Deere tractor. For many years, they have had the same colors— green bodies with yellow trim. Many farmers are loyal Deere customers. They wouldn't use any other brand of tractor. There is even a John Deere tractor collectors club. This is called the Two-Cylinder Club, because at one time all Deere tractors had two-cylinder engines.

John Deere's recent 8000-series tractors have engines that range from 160 to 225 PTO horsepower. They have sixteen forward speeds and four reverse speeds. As an option, the company also offers a three-point hitch on the front of the four 8000-series tractors.

Deere has also come up with a new cab design, which it calls the CommandView cab. The engine and transmission sit in a narrow space, and the engine sits over the front axle. This gives the driver in the car a much better view of the wheels and ground. It also gives the tractor better balance.

Kubota

This Canadian company has designed a special four-wheel-drive tractor for use in vineyards and orchards. This model, the M7030DTN-B, has a steering system that speeds up the front wheels as the tractor turns. This makes the machine easy to turn at the end of a row of trees, vines, or bushes.

Farmers use the Kubota for spraying, seeding, and cultivating orchards. With sixteen forward gears and four reverse gears, the tractor can work in different conditions and on different types of ground. It is easy to till the ground or do snowplowing with the tractor's creeper speeds.

Massey-Ferguson

This Canadian business began as the Massey-Harris Company in 1891. In the 1950s, it combined with Harry Ferguson, Inc., a

Combines are tractors that can harvest and process grain crops such as wheat or corn.

business named for the inventor of the three-point hitch.

Two of the most famous Massey tractors were the Junior Twin Power and the Massey-Harris Pony. The Super Row Crop, which first came out in the 1930s, had side panels that completely enclosed the engine.

Chapter 5

Driverless Tractors

Many inventors have tried to create a tractor that can work without a human operator. A team of English inventors developed the first driverless tractor in the 1950s. This machine ran on electric current. Underground wires carried the current. A sensor on the tractor followed the current, and a hydraulic system steered the tractor.

The English driverless tractor worked as an experiment. But it wasn't very practical. A human driver can spot rocks and other dangers in the field. And only a human can make the small adjustments that are often necessary while driving a tractor.

Newer Models

Inventors have not stopped trying to make a driverless tractor. There are problems that driverless machines might help to solve. When heavy tractors press down the soil, for example, rain and fertilizer run off the land, instead of going to the plants that need them. A lighter machine might not create runoff.

This John Deere diesel tractor has an unusual shape.

In the 1980s, a Finnish company, Kone
Sampo, built two models of a lightweight,
driverless tractor—the Module and the
Modulaire. The Module has wide wheels, and
the Modulaire uses rubber tracks. Video
cameras on the tractors send a picture to the
operator, who controls the speed and turns the
machines with a radio signal.

In 1994, the company designed an automatic
navigation system. Signal beacons in the field

guide the tractor along the rows. A computer stores information on the size of the field. The computer also knows where hills and obstacles are. With this machine, the Module and the Modulaire can work automatically.

Into the Future

Many of today's tractors have new devices to make the farmer's job easier. Monitors in the cabs, for example, can check the amount of seed or fertilizer that a farmer is spreading on his fields. During the harvest, monitors can also measure the quantity of crop that has been gathered.

Today's tractors offer drivers greater comfort than tractors did in the past. Many models come with air-conditioned cabs, stereo sound systems, power steering, power brakes, and even beverage warmers. Farmers are still working hard, but modern tractors are helping them to work better and faster.

Glossary

crawler tractor—a tractor that moves on endless tracks that loop around the wheels

creeper gears—transmission speeds that allow the tractor to move very slowly without stalling

cultivate—to loosen, break up, and prepare the soil for planting and growing crops

drawbar—a beam used for attaching implements, tools, or wagons to the back of a tractor

driveshaft—a device that transmits power to the implement attached to a tractor

fertile—able to nourish vegetation, such as crops

fertilizer—a substance that helps soil become more fertile

horsepower—a measure of engine strength. One horsepower equals the strength to move 550 pounds (250.4 kilograms) one foot (30 centimeters) per second.

hydraulic system—a set of pumps and fluid-filled cylinders that power different parts of a tractor as well as implements and hitches

implement—machines used for farming jobs like planting, cultivating, mowing, and harvesting

internal-combustion engine—a device that generates power from small explosions within an engine chamber

power takeoff—a system that runs an implement by transferring power from a tractor's engine

row-crop tractors—vehicles that can work crops planted in rows

shuttle-shift reverser—a transmission device that allows the driver to quickly change from forward to reverse gears

synchronized transmission—a transmission design that allows a smooth shift from one speed to the next

three-point hitch—a device that links implements to the back of a tractor. The three-point hitch transfers weight from the implement to the rear tires or tracks, allowing the tractor to get more traction.

traction—the friction created by a wheel or track moving along the ground. The greater the traction, the more power that is available to the implement for work.

To Learn More

Bushey, Jerry. *Farming the Land: Modern Farmers and Their Machines.* Minneapolis: Carolrhoda Books, 1987.

Williams, Michael. *Great Tractors.* Poole, Dorset, England: Blandford Press, 1982.

Young, Miriam Burt. *If I Drove a Tractor.* New York: Lothrop, Lee & Shepard, 1973.

Zim, Herbert Spencer and James R. Skelly. *Tractors.* New York: Morrow, 1972.

You can read articles about modern tractors and antique tractors in *Successful Farming Magazine, Antique Power Magazine, Farm Antiques News,* and *The Hook.*

Some Useful Addresses

Two-Cylinder Club
P.O. Box 219
Grundy Center, IA 50638-0219

Ford/Fordson Collectors Association
645 Loveland
Miamiville Rd.
Loveland, OH 45140

Intl. Harvester Collectors Association
RR 2, Box 286
Winamac, IN 46996

J.I. Case Collectors Association
Rt. 2, Box 242
Vinton, OH 45686-9741

Index

Allis-AGCO, 30-31
Allis-Chalmers, 29

brakes, 24, 27, 42

Caterpillar Company, 29, 32
Challenger tractors, 32-33
crawlers, 25-26
Crossmotor tractors, 31

drawbars, 16
driverless tractors, 39-42

8000-series tractors, 34
engines, 6, 12, 15, 21, 31, 33-34
Farmall tractors, 17
Ferguson, Henry, 18
fertilizer, 5, 40, 42
Ford Motor Company, 13, 29, 33

Fordson tractor, 13, 33
four-wheel drive, 26
Froehlich, John, 12

Genesis tractors, 33-34

Hart, Charles, 12
Hart-Parr tractors, 12
hydraulic systems, 21, 24, 39

International Harvester, 17

J.I. Case Company, 29, 31
John Deere Company, 29, 34

Kone Sampo, 41-42
Kubota tractors, 36

Magnum tractors, 31

Parr, Charles, 12

plows, 6, 26
power steering, 24, 27, 42
power takeoffs, 15-16, 26, 30

roll bars, 27
row-crop tractors, 16-17

soil, 5-6, 20, 26, 32
sprayers, 26
steam tractors, 11-12

three-point hitch, 18-19, 21
tires, 20, 26, 32
traction, 19-20
transmissions, 6, 30, 34
Two-Cylinder Club, 34

wheels, 16, 19-21, 24, 33, 36
Winnipeg, Canada, 12